arcola
theatre

Arcola Theatre presents

MARE RIDER
by Leyla Nazli

First performed at Arcola Theatre, 22 January 2013

The Peggy Ramsay Foundation

EUROPE NOW

Columbia Foundation Fund
of the Capital Community Foundation

Supported using public funding by
**ARTS COUNCIL
ENGLAND**

LOTTERY FUNDED

MARE RIDER
by Leyla Nazli

CAST

Mark	Matthew Flynn
Selma	Anna Francolini
Elka	Kathryn Hunter
Claire	Hara Yannas

PRODUCTION TEAM

Directed by	Mehmet Ergen
Design	Matthew Wright
Lighting Design	Richard Williamson
Video Design	Ben Walden and Dick Straker for MESMER
Music and Sound Design	Neil McKeown
Assistant Director	Natalie Katsou
Movement Director	Nathan M. Wright
Costume Supervisor	Alice Walkling
Production Manager	Vivienne Clavering
Press Representative	Cliona Roberts PR cliona@crpr.co.uk 020 7704 6224
Production Photography	Simon Annand

FOR ARCOLA THEATRE

Leyla Nazli (Writer)
Leyal Nazli's first play **Silver Birch House** (Oberon Books, 2007) was staged by Mehmet Ergen to critical acclaim at Arcola Theatre. This followed a rehearsed reading at the Royal Court Theatre in 2006, where Leyla was one of 50 writers chosen to take part in The Fifty, a year-long project with the BBC to celebrate the 50th anniversary of the theatre. Her credits as adaptor include Gogol's **The Government Inspector** and credits as translator include Kroetz's **The Nest**. Leyla co-founded Arcola Theatre with Mehmet Ergen in 2000, where she has been Executive Producer since 2004.

CAST

Matthew Flynn (Mark)
Matthew trained at Drama Centre, London.
Theatre includes: **55 Days** (Hampstead Theatre); **Henry V** and **Troilus and Cressida** (Shakespeare's Globe); **A Streetcar Named Desire** (Liverpool Playhouse); **The Two Gentlemen of Verona** (Northampton); **Macbeth** and **The Mayor of Zalamea** (Liverpool Everyman); **As You Like It**, **Macbeth** and **How Many Miles to Basra?** (West Yorkshire Playhouse); **1984** and **Julius Caesar** (Royal Exchange, Manchester); **The Gentleman's Tea Drinking Society** (Ransom, Tron Theatre); **Hangover Square** (Finborough Theatre); **Our Friends in the North** (Northern Stage); **The Winter's Tale** (Propeller, BAM New York International Tour); **Romeo and Juliet** (Derby Playhouse); **A Midsummer Night's Dream** (Propeller, Comedy Theatre, BAM New York World Tour); **A View from the Bridge** (National Tour); **Rose Rage** (Propeller, Theatre Royal Haymarket, International Tour); **The**

Prince of Homburg (RSC, Lyric Theatre); **Meat** (Theatre Royal, Plymouth); **Hamlet** (Bristol Old Vic); **Twelfth Night** (Propeller, Watermill Theatre); **The Comedy of Errors** (Propeller, International Tour); **Henry V** (Propeller, International Tour); **Julius Caesar** (Royal Exchange, Manchester); **Romeo and Juliet** and **Julius Caesar** (RSC) and **An Ideal Husband** (Gielgud Theatre, Peter Hall Company). Television includes: **Holby City**, **The Passion**, **Midsomer Murders**, **Coronation Street**, **After Thomas**, **The Quartermass Experiment**, **Foyles War**, **Doctors**, **Trial and Retribution** and **A Class Act**. Film includes: **Franklyn**, **Sahara** and **The Final Passage**.

Anna Francolini (Selma) Theatre includes: **Victor/ Victoria** (Southwark Playhouse); **How The World Began** (Arcola Theatre); **A View From The Bridge** (Royal Exchange Theatre); **Onassis** (Novello Theatre); **Taking Steps** (Orange Tree Theatre); **The Prime of Miss Jean Brodie** (Northampton Royal Theatre and Edinburgh, TMA Award Best Performance in a Play); **Awaking Beauty** (Stephen Joseph Theatre); **Wolves at the Window** (Arcola and 59E59 Theater, New York); **Three Sisters on Hope Street** (Liverpool Everyman and Hampstead); **Alphabetical Order** (Salisbury Playhouse); **In The Club** (Hampstead); **Into The Woods** (Royal Opera House); **Caroline, Or Change** (National Theatre, Olivier Award Nomination); **Anatol** (Arcola); **Six Pictures Of Lee Miller** (Minerva, Chichester); **Spittin' Distance** (Stephen Joseph Theatre); **Romeo And Juliet** (English Touring Theatre); **Things You Shouldn't Say Past Midnight** (Soho); **Daisy Pulls It Off** (Lyric); **Mahler's Conversion**

(Aldwych); **Merrily We Roll Along** (Donmar Warehouse); **The Tempest** (A&BC); **The Ballad Of Little Jo, Floyd Collins** and **Saturday Night** (Bridewell); **A Midsummer Night's Dream** (Oxford Stage Company); **Metropolis Kabarett** (National Theatre); **Little Shop of Horrors** (Watermill); **Company** (Donmar Warehouse and Albery) and **Oliver!** (London Palladium).

Television includes: **EastEnders, Pixelface, Doctors, Live! Girls!, Rome, Holby City, Lie With Me, Down To Earth, This Is Dom Joly, Jonathan Creek, Company** and **Mash & Peas Do U.S.**

Film includes: **Topsy Turvy, The Final Curtain, The Barn** and **Z**.

Radio includes: **Ruth** and **David Golder** (First Writes Radio/BBC Radio 4).

Kathryn Hunter (Elka)
Recent theatre includes: Juliet in **Tender Thing** by Ben Power (Swan Theatre Stratford, directed by Helena Kaut-Howson; a laboratory production of **King Lear** with final year acting students from UCLA.

Previous theatre includes: Mr. Iao in **The Bee** by Hideki Noda and Colin Teevan (London, New York and Tokyo); **Spoonface Steinberg** by Lee Hall, directed by Annie Castledine and Marcello Magni; **The Skriker** by Caryl Churchill (Time Out Best Actress); Lear in **King Lear**, directed by Helena Kaut-Howson (The Young Vic and Tokyo); title role in **Richard III**, directed by Barry Kyle (Shakespeare's Globe); Clara Zachannassian in **The Visit**, directed by Annabel Arden (for Theatre de Complicite); **Anything for a Quiet Life** (theatre and film); **Women of Troy** directed by Katie Mitchell (Gate for Theatre de Complicite) and **Our Country's Good** by Timberlake Wertenbaker, directed by Max Stafford-Clark.

Forthcoming productions include: **My Perfect Mind** (Kathryn directs Paul Hunter and Edward Petherbridge in a co-production for Told By An Idiot at Plymouth Theatre Royal and The Young Vic); **Kafka's Monkey** and **Fragments** (TFNA New York); **Cards 2** with Robert LePage and Exmachina and **A Midsummer Night's Dream** (TFNA New York, directed by Julie Taymor).
Work as Director includes: **Puntila and His Man Matti** (Almeida, Traverse and Albery); **Glory of Living** by Rebecca Gilman (Royal Court); **The Birds** (National Theatre); **Pericles** and **Comedy of Errors** (Shakespeare's Globe)
Film includes: Sally Potter's **Orlando**, Mike Leigh's **All or Nothing** and Miss Figg in **Harry Potter and the Order of the Phoenix.**

Hara Yannas (Claire)
Hara trained at London Academy of Music and Dramatic Art (LAMDA). Theatre includes: **The House of Bernarda Alba** (Almeida Theatre); **Britannicus** (Wilton's Music Hall); **Pericles** (Open Air Theatre, Regent's Park); **Uncle Vanya** (Arcola Theatre/Belgrade Theatre, Coventry); **it felt empty when the heart went at first but it is alright now** (Arcola Theatre/Clean Break) and **A Midsummer Night's Dream** (Shakespeare's Globe and Tour).
Television credits include: **The Bible** (History Channel) and **Holby City** (BBC).

PRODUCTION TEAM

Mehmet Ergen (Director)
Mehmet is founder and Artistic Director of both Arcola Theatre in London and Talimhane Theatre in Istanbul. He co-founded and was the first Artistic Director of the Southwark Playhouse between 1993 and 1999, before becoming Associate Producer of the Battersea Arts Centre from 1999 to 2001.

His directing work at Arcola includes: **The Painter** by Rebecca Lenkiewicz, **An Enemy of the People** by Henrik Ibsen, **Chasing the Moment** by Jack Shepherd, **The Plebeians Rehearse the Uprising** by Günter Grass, **Jitterbug** by Bonnie Greer, **A Midsummer Night's Dream** and **Macbeth** by William Shakespeare, as well as Leyla Nazli's first play, **Silver Birch House**.

His directing work elsewhere includes: **It Felt Empty...** by Lucy Kirkwood, **Dumb Show** by Joe Penhall, **Afterplay** by Brian Friel, **Noises Off** by Michael Frayn, **The Betrayal** by Harold Pinter, **The Pillowman** by Martin McDonagh, **Boy Gets Girl** by Rebecca Gilman, **The Shape of Things** by Neil LaBute, **Chicago** by Sam Shepard, **The Nest** by Franz Xaver Kroetz, **Much Ado About Nothing** and **King Lear** by William Shakespeare, **Roots** by Arnold Wesker, **Of Mice and Men** by John Steinbeck, **The Protagonist** by Georg Kaiser, **In the Jungle of the Cities, Informer, The Exception and the Rule** and **Senora Carrar's Rifles** by Bertolt Brecht, and **Mandragola** by Machiavelli. His work on operas and musicals include: **Sweet Smell of Success** by Marvin Hamlisch, Craig Carnelia and John Guare, **The Cradle Will Rock** by Marc Blitzstein, **Seven Deadly Sins** by Bertolt Brecht & Kurt Weill, **I Can Get It for You Wholesale** by Jerome Weidman & Harold Rome, **Treemonisha** by Scott Joplin and **Lost in the Stars** by Kurt Weill.

His translations include works by Miguel de Cervantes, Henrik Ibsen, Harold Pinter, Jack Shepard, Neil LaBute, Martin McDonagh and Enda Walsh.

He is an advisor and judge for BBC Radio drama, founder of Arcola's opera season **Grimeborn** and founder of the new writing festival, **Oyun Yaz**.

Natalie Katsou
(Assistant Director)
Natalie Katsou is a Theatre Director and Playwright. She was born in Athens. After her studies in Acting (Delos Acting School – BA Acting) and Theatre (University of

Athens – BA Theatre Studies), she completed her MFA in Theatre Directing in East15 Acting School (University of Essex) under the honorary Minotis Scholarship from the Cultural Foundation by the National Bank of Greece. She has also studied Law (University of Athens – Law Degree) and Piano (Maria Callas Conservatory). Her first directing role was for **The Wedding Dress** at the National Theatre of Greece in 2006. From 2006 to 2009 she was the Artistic Director of En Spoudi Fringe Co. Since 2010 she has lived and worked in London. She currently works as a director for Arcola Youth Theatre. Her directing work in UK includes: **Minotaur** (Space, Edinburgh Festival Fringe); **Rhinoceros** (Clifftown Theatre, Southend); **Bacchae** and **Antigone** (in Theatro Technis); and **do not feed the pigeons** (Roding House). Credits as Assistant Director: **Sweet Smell of Success** (Arcola, dir. Mehmet Ergen); **La Traviata** (Observantship, ROH London); **The Lark** and **A Midsummer Night's Dream** (Clifftown Theatre, Southend, dir. Chris Rolls); **The Visit** (Theatre Kefallinias, Athens, dir. Stathis Livathinos) and **Macbeth** (Tour, dir. George Kimoulis).

Neil McKeown (Music and Sound Design)
Neil has been producing music in one form or another for 15 years, but has recently been concentrating on sound design and composition for theatre.
His theatrical sound credits include sound director for the award-winning immersive theatrical production **You Me Bum Bum Train** and sound designer for Identity Drama School's Winter Showcases. This is a new and exciting development in his career, allowing him to explore his love of theatrical sound.

Benjamin Walden for **MESMER** (Video Design)
Benjamin's video design credits include **Jekyll & Hyde: The Musical** (Union Theatre) and **Kiss of the Spider Woman** (Arts Ed). Benjamin has also worked as Video Supervisor for **Lovesong** (Frantic Assembly, UK tour); **Macbeth** (National Theatre of Scotland, UK/US tour) and **Menage A Trois** (National Theatre of Scotland, UK tour).
He has also worked as Video Technician at the National Theatre. Productions there include **Fela!** (Olivier Theatre); **Beauty and the Beast** (Cottesloe Theatre) and **Greenland** (Lyttelton Theatre).
Benjamin is also an ongoing

associate of the video design collective, MESMER. As well as theatre and other live events, Benjamin works as a cameraman and editor for short films, music videos and documentaries.

Alice Walkling
(Costume Supervisor)
Alice graduated from the Motley Theatre Design Course in 2005. She works as a Costume Designer and Supervisor in Theatre, Television and Film.
Recent projects include **Boy Meets Boy** (Jermyn Street Theatre); **Is that a Bolt in Your Neck?** (Pleasance Theatre and touring); **The House of Atreus** (Guildhall School of Music and Drama); **The Black Diamond** (Punchdrunk and Stella Artois); **Casting Traces** (New Movement Collective); **Cartoonito Tales** (Cartoon Network) and **Jam Tomorrow** (Linbury Studios, ROH) choreographed by Kristen McNally.
Alice designed and made the costumes for Fitcher's **Bird and Heist**, choreographed by Jonathon Goddard and Gemma Nixon. She has also worked extensively in the costume departments of the Royal Opera House, Shakespeare's Globe and the Royal Shakespeare Company.
alicewalkling.com

Matthew Wright (Design)
Matthew's theatre design credits include **La Cage Aux Folles** (Menier Chocolate Factory/West End/Broadway/US tour) for which he received Drama Desk and Outer Critics Circle Awards for Outstanding Costume Design, Tony and Olivier Award nominations for Best Costume Design.
Other designs include **Sweet Charity** (Menier/West End); **Shadowlands** and **The Glass Menagerie** (West End); **Speaking Like Magpies** (RSC/West End, nominated for TMA Best Design Award); **Blackbird** (Market Theatre, Johannesburg); **In Praise of Love** (Chichester); **Road Show, They're Playing Our Song** and **The Invisible Man** (Menier Chocolate Factory); **Evita** (UK tour); **Brother Love's Travelling Salvation Show** (UK tour); **The Norman Conquests**, **Kes** (Liverpool); **A Man of No Importance**, **Stepping Out**, **A Month in the Country**, **Alphabetical Order**, **What The Butler Saw** (Salisbury); **A Song at Twilight** (Colchester/UK tour); **Clouds** (UK tour); **Larkin With Women** (WYP); **The Green Man** (Bush/Plymouth); **One Under** (Tricycle); **US and Them, The Dead Eye Boy** (Hampstead) and **Behzti** (Birmingham Rep).

Nathan M. Wright
(Movement Director)
London Choreographic
credits: **Sweet Smell of
Success** (Arcola Theatre),
What's On Stage Nomination
– Best Choreography in
a Musical, The Offies, Off
West End Nomination – Best
Choreography in a Musical,
The Rocky Horror Show 40th
Anniversary Production (ATG)
and **The Tailor Made Man.**
Nathan was a Mass
Movement Choreographer
on The Opening and
Closing Ceremonies for
both **The London 2012
Olympic & Paralympic
Games, The Delhi 2010
Commonwealth Games
Handover Ceremony, Oman
National Day, The 2010
Winter Olympics Vancouver,
Canada** – Segment Director
Closing Ceremony Finale
and Michael Bublé – Closing
Ceremony, **The 2007 Special
Olympics Shanghai** (Athlete's
Parade) and **The 15th Asian
Games Doha, Qatar**.
Australian choreographic
credits: **Avenue Q** (Helpmann
Award Nomination – Best
Choreography, Green Room
Award Nomination – Best
Choreography), **Gutenberg!
The Musical** (Helpmann
Award Nomination – Best
Choreography) For The
STC – **Not Quite Out Of
The Woods** and **Pennies'
from Kevin. David
Campbell – On Broadway
Tour, Side by Side by
Sondheim, The Shakespeare
Revue, Lovebites, Breast
Wishes, Boeing-Boeing,
Showstoppers**.
Film: The Wicked Faced Boy
in Baz Luhrmann's **Moulin
Rouge**, Motion Capture
Artist on Award-winning
film **Happy Feet** and most
recently Nathan was The
Associate Choreographer on
Baz Luhrmann's **The Great
Gatsby**.
www.nathanmwright.com

A very special thanks to the following for their involvement with **Mare Rider** from its inception.

Rebecca Lenkiewicz
John Burgess
Helena Kaut-Howson
Richard Walker
Vytautas Pocious
Zeynep Kepekli
Francois Langtom
Rei Kurosaki
David Todd
Luke Boffa
Katharine Armitage
Samantha Young
Andrew Whipp
Alicia Davies
Miranda (the mare on the poster)
Melody Brown

WRITER'S NOTE

This play draws on the Elka myth which is prevalent, amongst other places, in Eastern Turkey. The myth and associated traditions might be interpreted as a way of addressing perinatal and postpartum (postnatal) depression. It also captures many other folkloric themes from earlier and geographically distant cultures relating to powerful women, horses and mysticism which may have found their way to contemporary East Turkey.

Whilst the accurate history or analysis of these themes is far from my intention with this play, I thought it might be useful to share some of my background notes on them. These ad-hoc notes have been chopped and changed from a variety of sources and are presented in no particular order.

The Amazons were said to have lived in Pontus, which is part of modern day Turkey near the shore of the Black Sea. There they formed an independent kingdom under the government of a queen named Hippolyte which might be translated as 'loose, unbridled mare'.

The banshee, woman of the fairy mounds, is a female spirit in Irish mythology, usually seen as an omen of death and a messenger from the Otherworld who may begin to wail if someone is about to die. Similar beings are also found in Welsh, Norse and American folklore. The banshee can appear in a variety of guises. Most often she appears as an ugly, frightening hag, but she can also appear as a stunningly beautiful woman of any age that suits her.

Jung is quoted as having said the horse represents 'the mother within us' explaining that the animal has a power understanding, intuition and magical side that is distinctive from anything else in nature. In ancient Greece the horse was worshipped and prized as a special possession being associated with the Goddess Artemis.

Lady Godiva took pity on the people of Coventry, who were suffering grievously under her husband's oppressive taxation. He said he would grant her request to lessen taxes if she would strip naked and ride through the streets of the town. Some historians have discerned elements of pagan fertility rituals in the Godiva story whereby a young 'May Queen' was led to the sacred Cofa's tree perhaps to celebrate the renewal of spring.

Lilith, a Hebrew name for a figure in Jewish mythology, is generally thought to be in part derived from a class of female demons in Mesopotamian texts. In the 8th-10th Century Lilith is identified as Adam's first wife, who was created at the same time and from the same earth as Adam. This contrasts with Eve, who was created from one of Adam's ribs. Lilith claims that since she and Adam were created in the same way they were equal and she refuses to submit to him. Later myths of Lilith involve another world, existing side-by-side with this one, with Lilith as the queen of Asmodeus, King of Demons. Many disasters are blamed on both of them, causing wine to turn into vinegar, men to be impotent, women unable to give birth, and it was Lilith who was blamed for the loss of infant life.

Stockholm syndrome, or capture-bonding, is a psychological phenomenon in which hostages express empathy, sympathy and have positive feelings towards their captors, sometimes to the point of defending them. These feelings are generally considered irrational in light of the danger or risk endured by the victims, who essentially mistake a lack of abuse from their captors for an act of kindness.

The popularity of coffee engendered great controversy throughout the first few centuries of its history in the Islamic world. Many were suspicious of the effects of caffeine and the gatherings in which it was consumed – they seemed debauched to some and subversive to others. Efforts were launched, and persisted for at least a hundred years, to declare coffee an intoxicant forbidden by Islamic law. Similarly, Pope Clement VIII was asked by his advisers to ban coffee as it was a favourite beverage of the Ottoman Empire, part of that infidel threat, and the 'drink of the devil' condemned by the Roman clergy.

London, January 2013

MARE RIDER

Leyla Nazli

MARE RIDER

OBERON BOOKS
LONDON

WWW.OBERONBOOKS.COM

First published in 2013 by Oberon Books Ltd
521 Caledonian Road, London N7 9RH
Tel: +44 (0) 20 7607 3637 / Fax: +44 (0) 20 7607 3629
e-mail: info@oberonbooks.com
www.oberonbooks.com

A catalogue record for this book is available from the British
Library.

PB ISBN: 978-1-84943-430-0
E ISBN: 978-1-84943-930-5

Cover image by Simon Annand

Printed, bound and converted
by CPI Group (UK) Ltd, Croydon, CR0 4YY.

Visit www.oberonbooks.com to read more about all our books
and to buy them. You will also find features, author interviews and
news of any author events, and you can sign up for e-newsletters
so that you're always first to hear about our new releases.

Characters

MARK

SELMA

ELKA

CLAIRE

Mare Rider was first performed at the Arcola Theatre, London on 22 January 2013 with the following cast and crew:

MARK	Matthew Flynn
SELMA	Anna Francolini
ELKA	Kathryn Hunter
CLAIRE	Hara Yannas

Directed by Mehmet Ergen

Designer Matthew Wright

Lighting Designer Richard Williamson

Sound Designer Neil MacKeown

Video Design Ben Walden and Dick Straker (MESMER)

Costume Supervisor Alice Walking

Assistant Director Natalie Katsou

SCENE 1

SELMA is in hospital. It's evening. There is music in the background, which sounds almost like a wailing woman. We hear a galloping horse sound as ELKA enters and goes to SELMA's bed.

ELKA: Hi.

SELMA: Hi.

    What was that?

ELKA: What?

SELMA: I thought I heard a horse.

ELKA: In a hospital?

SELMA: Are you my doctor?

ELKA: No.

SELMA: Or the nurse?

ELKA: No.

    Queer quietness.

SELMA: You're here for a birth then.

    ELKA smiles.

ELKA: It's a bit late for me. Don't you think?

SELMA: Technology is so advanced these days.

ELKA: I wasn't lucky enough to catch the technology.

SELMA: I'm sorry to hear that.

ELKA: I don't understand it.

SELMA: It changes so quickly. As soon as I learn how to use all the functions in my mobile, they update the phone again. I can't keep up.

ELKA: Do you like it?

SELMA: Yes and no.

ELKA: Start with why you like it.

SELMA: I like it because I can reach Mark any time I want. Where's he?

ELKA: I take it Mark is your husband?

SELMA: Yes.

ELKA: Do you call your husband all the time?

SELMA: I call him when I need him.

ELKA: And he grants your wishes immediately?

SELMA: Whenever he can.

ELKA: Did you call him tonight?

SELMA: No, I didn't.

ELKA: Did he call you?

SELMA: We aren't allowed to use mobiles in the hospital.

ELKA: But he can call you on the landline.

SELMA: I suppose he can. Perhaps he did and the nurse forgot to tell me.

ELKA: You don't have to find excuses for him.

SELMA: Are you always this direct with people you don't know?

ELKA: He just left you to me to deal with.

SELMA: What?

I'm sorry I think I need to rest now.

ELKA: Ignore it. The modern world's solution for everything. Just ignore it.

SELMA: He didn't know I was going to spend the night here.

ELKA: You nearly died.

SELMA: We're not in the dark ages. How do you know this anyway?

ELKA: Did you think you'd go home straight after?

SELMA: Why all these questions? Who are you?

ELKA: Don't be pissed off.

SELMA: Please go back to your bed.

ELKA: I don't have a bed.

SELMA: To your ward then. To wherever you came from.

ELKA: You don't have to be like this. I thought you needed to talk with someone.

SELMA: I don't. What time is it?

ELKA: I don't know. I don't like time.

SELMA: Clearly.

ELKA: For me, time is now.

SELMA: Now she thinks she is timeless.

ELKA: I am. You should know that.

SELMA: I should know what?

ELKA: You know me very well.

SELMA: I've never seen you before in my life.

ELKA: You didn't need to see me.

SELMA: Are you one of Mark's relatives?

ELKA: What makes you think that I am related to him?

SELMA: I don't have any relatives in this country.

ELKA: I'm not related to anyone, especially not to your husband, who is not here with his wife.

SELMA: It's the hospital rules.

ELKA: Women always make excuses for men.

SELMA: You don't know me.

ELKA: I know women better than anyone.

SELMA: Look, I'm not a mind-reader. Tell me who you are and stop this interrogation.

ELKA: Very well then.

She stares at SELMA, not quite sure how to explain.

SELMA: Well?

ELKA: I have travelled through the plateaus of Mongolia, over the mountains of Afghanistan, Kashmir, the rivers of India, beautiful Gardens of Babylon, crossing the deserts of Arabia, Mesopotamia the cradle of civilisation, now ruins of Anatolia, skipping over the magnificent Alps to the end of nowhere. Homerton Hospital in Hackney.

SELMA: I hate hospitals. There is always a lunatic and they always find me.

ELKA: Did you look really hard for this place?

What a shit hole.

SELMA: A hospital is a hospital, and I hate all of them.

ELKA: You're never out of them for some bizarre reason.

SELMA: What did you say?

ELKA: Nothing.

SELMA: What's your name?

ELKA: Elka.

Long pause.

You know that name very well.

SELMA: That can't be real.

ELKA: You didn't think I'd find you here, did you?

SELMA: I think I'm dreaming.

ELKA: Think what you like.

SELMA: Why are you here?

ELKA: Here we go.

SELMA: Nightmare Elka.

ELKA: I prefer just Elka.

SELMA: Nurse! Nurse!

ELKA: Don't waste your energy.

SELMA: Nurse!

ELKA: She can't hear you.

SELMA: What did you do to her?

ELKA: I've done nothing. She just can't be bothered with you.

SELMA: But this is her job.

ELKA: What, to attend to you every time you have a nightmare?

SELMA: Am I having a nightmare?

ELKA: Isn't that what you called me?

SELMA: Oh, that's good then.

ELKA: So, boy or girl?

> *No answer.*

> Talk to me.

SELMA: Why do you want to know?

ELKA: Boy.

SELMA: Why ask then?

ELKA: I'm trying to make a conversation.

SELMA: Please do not take him away from me.

ELKA: Or you from him.

SELMA: Take my heart, but please don't touch my baby.

ELKA: It's stupid to be a mother at your age.

SELMA: I needed to work. And, yes, I was stupid.

ELKA: Do you have any savings for this baby then?

SELMA: No.

ELKA: To wait all this time and not give him a secure future?

SELMA: No one has a secure future. That's what I understood,
eventually.

ELKA: Work. Career. All the things a modern woman wants.

SELMA: What's wrong with that?

ELKA: I think it's selfish.

SELMA: Do you think it's easy to survive in the twenty-first
century? You'd be swallowed up.

ELKA: By men?

SELMA: Not only by men, but by women also. Like you.

ELKA: What have I done?

SELMA: You know, when you throw crabs into boiling water,
the male crabs hold on to each other and try to climb up
by building a ladder, whereas the female crabs jump on
top of each other. I wonder why we're like that.

ELKA: That's what I've been wondering for thousands of years.

SELMA: And you couldn't find an answer in all that time?

ELKA: The answer is within you.

SELMA: Oh, please stop the wise wisdom crap. I don't need that.

ELKA: You're not in a position to talk to me like that.

ELKA makes her way towards the door.

SELMA: Where are you going? Please don't touch my baby. I beg you.

Please stop. Please stop.

ELKA slowly slips away. SELMA is in a panic.

I am sorry! Nurse! Nurse!

CLAIRE: What's the matter?

SELMA: Please check on my baby. He's in danger.

CLAIRE: Shshsh… Everyone is sleeping.

SELMA: My baby. She's taking my baby!

CLAIRE: You're disturbing the other mothers.

SELMA: You don't understand. I want to see my son now!

CLAIRE: Just calm down. I'll see what I can do.

SELMA: She…she's got my baby…

CLAIRE: No one has got your baby.

SELMA tries to get up. CLAIRE stops her.

SELMA: Get out of my way!

CLAIRE: You shouldn't make sudden moves.

SELMA passes out.

SCENE 2

Lights back on SELMA. ELKA is staring at her.

SELMA: What did you do to my baby?

ELKA: What do you think?

SELMA: Why is this happening to me?

> *SELMA tries to cry, but can't cry loud, despite trying very hard.*

ELKA: What name did you give him?

SELMA: We didn't have the chance, did we?

ELKA: Pity.

SELMA: Go away. You horrible, horrible, I don't even know what you are!

ELKA: Woman! I am a woman.

SELMA: Why? Why do this?

ELKA: Because you didn't forget me.

SELMA: You touch my baby, because I didn't forget you?

ELKA: I held him.

SELMA: You held him. How did it feel?

ELKA: Cold.

SELMA: Cold. Why cold? Didn't they wrap him properly?

ELKA: All babies are cold. At least the ones I hold anyway.

SELMA: Tell me, how's remembering someone a bad thing?

ELKA: I didn't say it's bad. This is how I reward those who remember me as a nightmare.

SELMA: I did not.

ELKA: You don't have a good memory, do you?

SELMA: But I didn't recognise you, which means I didn't remember you.

ELKA: Didn't you call your mother, before you checked in here?

SELMA: Yes, I did speak to my mum, about my dad and his health…

ELKA: And about me.

SELMA: How did you know?

ELKA: You were afraid.

SELMA: Mum couldn't fly because my dad's ill.

ELKA: That was an invitation.

SELMA: I'm not afraid of you.

Isn't there anyone here?

ELKA: Wouldn't your husband be handy right now? What do you think?

SELMA: Men. I remember now. Men can catch you. They apply beeswax to the backs of their horses so that you stick if you ride them, and they poke you with needles if you come near their wives and babies.

ELKA: What a load of bollocks.

SELMA: How then?

ELKA: You believe all that crap, the things they made up about me, for centuries?

SELMA: I remember they used to say, you ride horses through the night until they sweat to death.

ELKA: If I could steal one.

SELMA: No wonder men chase you.

ELKA: I wasn't allowed to ride, so I did it secretly at night, when everyone was asleep. I love horses and I loved a little ride from time to time. What's wrong with that?

SELMA: I can't imagine you loving anything.

ELKA: Listen, you little bitch, I didn't choose to be like this.

SELMA: All I want is to see my baby.

ELKA: I'm not stopping you.

SELMA: If you must take life, then take mine.

ELKA: You know I prefer little babies first.

SELMA: You're not a human. A human being wouldn't do such a thing.

ELKA: I'll take that as a joke, but it's not funny.

SELMA: Why hasn't one of those men killed you yet?

ELKA: Why kill me, when they can use me as a slave?

SELMA: How did you survive all these years? It's impossible.

ELKA: I'm a legendary woman my dear, and as you know, the legendary women never die. They just get perfected over the years, like a tasty bottle of red wine.

SELMA: Did you ever look at yourself in the mirror?

ELKA: I don't need to. I know I'm beautiful.

SELMA: You look like a scarecrow.

ELKA: Oh, you really aren't afraid of me anymore, are you?

SELMA: You could at least brush your hair.

ELKA: This is my style. I like to be this way.

SELMA: You look like a witch. Who would want you like this?

ELKA: And that's why I'm the scariest and most horrific woman in the world. The one woman all the wives should stay away from. If I go near them or their children, they will die. I won't eat anything but feast on the livers of the women and their newly born babies. I'm so ugly and disgusting that no man can marry me. I won't wash in the rose-scented water or comb my hair like the other little wives do. Instead I wanted to ride horses. Go horse racing, hunting. Climb the mountains. I wanted to swim in the sweet pure river water until my body was soft like cotton. Wine. I wanted to drink wine, smoke pipe. Oh, that ancient smell of pipe passing through, like an invisible lover sweeping my face gently and disappearing around the corner. I wanted to inhale the life out of that lover. Now you call it cigarette.

SELMA: Smoking is bad for you.

ELKA: That should be your last worry, honey.

I wanted to work, like you. Not just cook and look after their bastards and get ready for their beds and breathe their foul breath every night.

SELMA: What can I do to see my baby?

ELKA: If you want to see your baby, you learn how to listen.

SELMA: I have been listening.

ELKA: I just wanted to live!

SELMA: By taking life?

ELKA: I couldn't live any of my dreams with people. So I did it alone, at night. Not marrying and not making myself beautiful for men was the only way I could be free. Now and then I stole their wine and horses.

SELMA: You are a cheap thief.

ELKA: My first horse was a black mare. I rode her through the meadow one spring evening. The grass was tall and was softly touching my legs. It felt like being caressed by gentle hands while the mare was galloping under me. The warm

evening wind was in my hair, just the right strength, as if
it was my lover's fingers combing my hair. My chest filled
with the sweet smell of flowers, my heart was pounding
like an eagle ready to take off to the sky and fly, fly and
fly, until it no longer needed to flap its wings. Just gliding
through the cool air softly and gently. Then I was in the
forest. The mare stopped to breathe as if she was telling
me that she had picked the right spot for me. Safe and far
from men. I held up the amphora of wine to the sky, made
a toast to the stars that were watching me and I tasted
the fermented sweet grape juice for the first time. It went
through my throat like a dancing mermaid. I lay down to
the ground, closed my eyes and prayed that my life could
be this joyful all the time and that I would have a sign from
God to reassure me that my wish was granted. When I
opened them, all I could see was a crystal clear sky full of
stars, all gleaming and smiling as if they were playing with
me. I held out my hands and they started dancing through
my fingers, swimming like a stream of phosphorescence
in the sea, giggling at me, and when I tried to catch them,
they all ran away like shy sea horses galloping with their
little tentacles high in the sky until I could never touch
them. Staring at me from far above, like aliens from a
shining city that was forbidden for me to go to. But I was
still happy at that time with my black mare grazing in my
hair.

*SELMA has forgotten her state during ELKA's journey and is as happy
as ELKA was for a few moments.*

SELMA: Whose mare was it?

ELKA: My uncle's. I thought if I stole from a relative it'd be
fine. It's family. I danced myself to sleep in the forest. Next
day, my uncle found me with his ugly dog. He didn't say
anything, but bound my hands with a rope and made me
walk home behind the mare. He pushed me to the ground
at our doorstep. My mother and father and all my sisters
just watched. He kicked me and left. Not saying a word.
They all turned around and went inside. Only my baby

sister came to me. She wasn't aware what was going on. She untied my hands, but she too had to follow the rest of the family when she heard my father's voice.

Pause.

SELMA: You probably think I should feel sorry for you, but I don't.

ELKA: I don't expect anyone to feel sorry for me. Especially not you. I know the only reason you're listening to me is because you are terrified of me.

SELMA: If you know this, why this torture?

ELKA: Because I can.

SELMA: Go back to your fucking hell!

ELKA: My dear, I'm not in hell, but you are.

SELMA: So, you're going to torture me slowly before you take my baby?

ELKA: Relax!

Long pause.

I heard my dad beating my mother all night over what I did. My mother gave him seven girls and not one son. He always blamed her for that and beat her every chance he got, whether it was her fault or not. I slept in the barn with the animals that night. In the morning my mother told me that the arrangement had been made. I was to be wedded to my cousin, my uncle's son. The ugliest man in the village. His mother knew he couldn't find a decent wife. They wanted our big field for my dowry. The land must stay with the family my uncle said. I thought of killing myself, but I didn't want my mother to find me dead in the barn, so I stole my uncle's mare again. I rode all night. I wanted to go as far as I could and if I died in the deepest point of the forest, I would be eaten by wolves, bears, birds and they would never be able to find one bit of me. I hadn't realised my ugly cousin had been following me. Bad luck. Now I was his slave forever. He took me to their house and chained me up in the kitchen. That was my wedding. I was chained for two years. Now and then they'd move me around if they needed me to clean different parts of the house or the barn or to weed the allotment. One day I discovered a little bird amongst the weed in the allotment eating seeds. I was hungry. They hardly fed me anything. So I ate the weeds too. That day I was the happiest woman on earth, giggling non-stop. I must have eaten a lot of it. I was free like in the forest dancing under the stars. Only this time there were no stars, yet I felt invincible. My brain was like a racing horse. That night I slept so soundly. Next evening I cooked spinach soup and put a ton of weed in it and served it for dinner.

SELMA: You drugged them.

ELKA: Wouldn't you, if Mother Nature had offered you such a gift?

SELMA: I have been listening to you all this time. Now can I see my baby?

ELKA: Do you want me to fetch him for you?

SELMA: Yes. No!

ELKA: Make your mind up.

SELMA: I want the nurse to bring my baby to me.

Nurse!

ELKA: I told you, no one cares about your stupid nightmares. Not even your mother.

SELMA: Keep my mother out of this.

ELKA: I visited her. When she was giving birth to your little sister. If your dad hadn't been there she would have had a heart attack. Didn't she tell you?

SELMA: She was hallucinating.

ELKA: You don't believe that.

SELMA: You're not real.

ELKA: I don't have to prove to you whether I'm real or not. That's not what I'm here for.

SELMA: You're here to murder.

ELKA is frustrated.

ELKA: I'm here to tell my story! I was a person. I am a person! A human being!

SELMA: And what makes you think people care about your story? There are so many things happening in the world every second. Who cares about your stupid little past life?

ELKA: Maybe. Maybe.

Short pause.

Don't you want to hear how I escaped the ugly husband?

SELMA: I do not. Stop playing with me.

ELKA: Well, you don't have a choice.

SELMA: Don't you think you're enslaving me the way they did you?

ELKA: I don't think it's the same at all. You're not scraping the floor or cooking for the most disgustingly mannered husband and mother-in-law. You're in bed listening to a bedtime story and you're not starving.

SELMA lets out a cry, but she can't move. Her body is numb.

SELMA: Aaaaaaargh!

ELKA: Don't wear yourself out.

SELMA: You promised me.

ELKA: No, I didn't.

SELMA: You said if I listened.

ELKA: And have you?

SELMA: I can't move.

ELKA: Here, smell this.

ELKA takes something from her bushy hair and holds it in front of SELMA's nose.

SELMA: You're drugging me.

ELKA: This is a mountain flower that takes its scent from a certain woman. She was pregnant when she was banished from her village and gave birth alone in the mountains. She wiped her forehead with this flower during birth. Since that day this flower holds her scent and always stays fresh, even when it's picked. You're very lucky. I don't use it often. Better?

SELMA is relaxed.

SELMA: Mmmmm. And the ugly husband?

ELKA: I drugged him. And my uncle and his wife. Later that evening, my husband came down to the kitchen to have me. I could see it in his grin. So I teased him a bit. He came up to me all giggly and wobbly, hardly standing on his feet. He fell on the ground just before reaching me.

SELMA: Your first kill.

ELKA: I didn't kill him. I just put him to sleep. I took the keys from around his neck. He always wore the key around his neck and said that he felt me near to his heart that way. So I spat on his heart. I took the mare once more and left for good. After two years I was free.

Lights down.

SCENE 3

Lights up. SELMA is sleeping. CLAIRE is on the phone talking to MARK.

CLAIRE: No, she didn't ask for you, but she wanted to see the baby. It can happen. A little hallucination is normal after what she's been through, but she went to sleep after I gave her something. No, don't worry. It's up to you if you'd like to pop in, but you can't stay long. Very well then. Of course I will pass your message on. Good night.

CLAIRE checks on SELMA and listens to her pulse. She takes her blood pressure and goes to check on other patients.

SELMA: Nurse. Nurse, was that you?

ELKA is holding SELMA's wrist, counting.

ELKA: Your husband called.

SELMA: Did he?

ELKA: He spoke to the nurse.

SELMA: And she didn't wake me up?

ELKA: Nurses won't wake the patient unless it's for medication.

SELMA: No one knows you're here, do they?

ELKA: No, they don't.

Pause.

SELMA: He didn't bother to come.

ELKA: It's nearly morning.

SELMA: He was probably exhausted.

ELKA: Or was with his mates.

SELMA: He should've been with me.

ELKA: Give the man a break.

SELMA: You wouldn't understand.

ELKA: You're just like any other woman.

SELMA: Here, stuck with you.

ELKA: Come on, having me around is not that bad.

SELMA: You always have been an unwanted guest and will always be one.

ELKA: Do you remember your cousin's birth?

SELMA: I didn't want to go to sleep that night. Now I want to sleep forever.

ELKA: You thought you could stay up all night.

SELMA: I was so curious to see what grown-ups did, but partly I was afraid to go to sleep just in case you came and took my cousin away. Eventually Mum gave up and I stayed with my sister and her friends.

ELKA: To keep me away.

SELMA: I discovered my sister had a boyfriend that night. I was sitting on the floor between the two of them, leaning against my sister. She put her arm around me but not holding me. Her hand just dropped on the floor behind me, then I realised she was holding his hand. They didn't look at each other and probably thought they were being very careful. My parents would have killed him if they knew about that, of course.

ELKA: No, they wouldn't. That was the point. Staying up with the mother and the newly born baby for three days and three nights was part of the fun. It was the only time young people could flirt and get to know each other in small villages. They have me to thank for that.

SELMA: All the girls were jealous of her. I thought she was the most beautiful girl and he was the most handsome boy in the world.

ELKA: Until the next morning, of course.

SELMA: I hated him. I hated both of them for doing that to me. He said it was one of their friends, but they could have stopped whoever did it.

ELKA: You knew the rules. No sleeping until dawn.

SELMA: It was so embarrassing trying to get up with cushions and duvets sewn all over me.

ELKA: You looked ridiculous with your moustache and beard.

SELMA: Mum had to rub it off really hard.

ELKA: But it was fun, wasn't it?

SELMA: I was ready to fight you if you did something to my cousin or my aunt.

ELKA: The hardest thing for me was to take a woman's life.

SELMA: How many have you killed?

ELKA: Oh, millions.

SELMA: Did you ever think of giving it up?

ELKA: It's not a job. I'm not doing it for fun either.

SELMA: Why then?

ELKA: The first time was out of desperation. After I lost the mare, running away was the only thing I could do. I ran, ran and ran until I could no longer be seen by anyone. Always hiding in the forest. The forest was my shield. Trying not to get caught, not to be prey for the animals was exhausting and I was always hungry. I didn't know how to hunt. Women weren't taught how to. I lived on grass, berries. Sometimes drinking milk from goats, cows, whatever I could find, but I had to be very careful. It wasn't easy. The shepherds were watching their animals like eagles and there were dogs.

One day I came to this small village. I thought now that I was far away from home no one would recognise me. Perhaps they would feel sorry for me and give me some food. I walked into the first house that was a half a mile away from the rest of the village. There was no one in. I went in to the kitchen to find some food, but there was nothing to eat. The family must have been very poor. Then I saw a bed on the floor. A woman sleeping with a newly born baby next to her. She has just been feeding the baby and they both fell asleep. Her breasts were out and were still full of milk. I couldn't resist. I started sucking her milk.

SELMA: You fed on baby's milk. Leaving him to starve.

ELKA: You've never suffered hunger have you?

SELMA doesn't answer this.

ELKA: I wasn't going to drink it all. Just a little to keep me alive. Then her husband came back from hunting. He dropped the deer on the floor and started shouting while I was enjoying my feast. 'God, please, keep us safe from life-sucking Elka'. The woman was screaming, the baby was crying, the husband was chasing me. I picked up his gun and ran, before he could catch me, leaving the dead mother and the crying baby. Since that day I was named life-sucking Elka and became the nightmare of women, including you.

SELMA: I never believed it.

ELKA: Yet you're afraid of me. All women fear each other.

SELMA: I think you should give some credit to modern women, because we have managed to improve quite a bit since then.

ELKA: I don't remember how many times I was enslaved by men. Sometimes women took pity on me and let me go. Sometimes they got jealous of their husbands and were equally horrible, but I never gave in. Never allowed them to take the sparks of the shining stars away from me. No matter how distant they were.

SELMA: I worked for 20 years to be able to stand on my own two feet. It took me 20 years to have a baby that I can't even hold.

ELKA: What happened to the fighting girl?

SELMA: Constant fight. Fight for job, for life, fight for air. I am so tired.

ELKA: You wouldn't want to raise your child in this world. Would you?

SELMA: We live in a time when we think we're free. In reality we have to think ten times more before saying anything.

ELKA: Holding thoughts makes people ill.

SELMA: What's your suggestion? To live alone in the forest like you?

ELKA: Yes. I can recommend you the perfect place.

SELMA: I bet it doesn't exist anymore.

ELKA: You're probably right about that.

SELMA: The most frustrating thing is people's untrusting silence. They don't say much, but find you weird if you have an opinion. There is no space for a mistake. You always have to wear this invisible mask that hides your real thoughts and rescues you from a disaster. It's a double-edged sword.

20 years! That's how long it took me to make my mind up in this modern world that we think is offering us everything.

ELKA: You're more of a slave than I was.

SELMA: I wouldn't go that far.

ELKA: What is that thing you're tapping at, like chicken eating corn, all day?

SELMA: Computer.

ELKA: You suffer from neck pain, back pain; gain weight by eating piles of sandwiches on that thing. Rushing like mad cows to pick up your children from school, fighting with your husbands who didn't bother to shift their arses from their computer while their women are constantly racing with time to put the children in bed.

SELMA: Men are in the same boat.

ELKA: I am talking about women. You only see your own small world, that is not wider than the screen of that computer, and prefer to shut your eyes on what's really happening. I don't.

SELMA: I used to think: the world is in deep shit. We must do something. Now when I hear about a political conflict in any part of the world, I pray to God that nobody does anything about it. Interfering with the wound, delays the healing. The best thing is to let it sort itself out.

ELKA: Do you really believe that?

SELMA: Most epidemics are cured in time when left to nature. So, perhaps it will take time for people to find their own solutions and, if along the way they suffer, then they suffer. At least they won't be cheated by an imported democracy like a sparkling golden chain as a promise to heaven's gate.

ELKA: Very good.

SELMA: I was in this business seminar once, on how to increase the sales of the company. The chairman talked all day and, at some point he said 'Listen, everyone thinks it's he who digs the gold who becomes rich; but that's not true. It's who sells it makes the money. And that's us. The man who owns the shovel. Nobody needs the gold digger, once the gold is dug'. And this other guy shouts out 'and we should always be the ones keeping the shovels afterwards'. I wanted to say: 'Yea, to bury the gold diggers', but I couldn't.

ELKA: I think I'm beginning to like you.

SELMA: I always think, if I can't change the world, my child
will, one day.

Where is my baby?

Blackout.

SCENE 4

SELMA is sleeping. CLAIRE and MARK are talking. It is 4.30 a.m.

CLAIRE: I had to give her a small amount of sedative.

MARK: Was she in pain?

CLAIRE: No, I think she was having a nightmare. It helped her to sleep.

MARK: I shouldn't wake her?

CLAIRE: No. You wouldn't want to cause problems for me, would you?

MARK: It would make her happy if she knew I was here.

CLAIRE: You can wait a while and see if she wakes up.

MARK: Really? I thought I couldn't.

CLAIRE: Technically you can't, but I'll let you get away with it this time.

MARK: That's very nice of you.

MARK goes to SELMA. He stares at her for a while. Then he strokes her hair and kisses on the forehead.

CLAIRE: *(Very quietly.)* You shouldn't wake her really. It took me a while to calm her down.

MARK: Sorry.

CLAIRE: Sit down.

MARK sits on a chair.

MARK: Thank you.

CLAIRE: How long have you been married?

MARK: Ten years.

CLAIRE: Fantastic.

MARK: Is it?

CLAIRE: My best friend Shirley met her husband when she was 22, and they're still together after five years.

MARK: Really?

CLAIRE: I admire them. They fight a lot though.

MARK: Right.

CLAIRE: Over the dinner, dog…you name it. The kids…

MARK: That's marriage for you.

CLAIRE: I've always thought I'll adopt one day.

MARK: That's a very noble thing to do.

CLAIRE: I know. There are so many children in the world with no parents and here we are, demanding a child from our own flesh and blood. What a selfish thing to do!

MARK: That's what we humans do. Reproduce.

CLAIRE: I didn't mean you at all. God, it all came out wrong.

MARK: No, don't feel bad.

CLAIRE: That's what I used to think, of course.

MARK: You don't think like that anymore?

CLAIRE: Stupid biological clock changed everything.

MARK: Right.

CLAIRE: It's like you're in a race and you need to finish it in two seconds. Now or never.

MARK: Pretty intense, ha.

CLAIRE: Oh, you men are so lucky!

Pause.

I'm sure your wife went through the same thing.

MARK: She never told me.

CLAIRE: I thought married people told each other everything.

MARK: Up to a point.

CLAIRE: What point is that then?

MARK: I don't know. There are certain things that you'd never share with anyone. They're just for you.

CLAIRE: Wow! Married for ten years and you still keep things from each other?

MARK: Everyone needs some privacy.

CLAIRE: In the toilet!

MARK: Would you like a cup of coffee? I think I need something to drink.

CLAIRE: Or I can make you a cup here, but it's instant.

MARK: No, no, I'll go to the café downstairs. What do you want?

CLAIRE: Latte please.

MARK: I'll be back in a sec. Will you tell my wife that I'm here if she wakes up?

CLAIRE: Of course I will.

MARK leaves. CLAIRE goes to check on other patients in the meantime.

SCENE 5

SELMA: Mark. Mark. I need to go to the toilet. Please, can you come to the toilet with me?

ELKA: Mark is not here.

SELMA: You again.

ELKA: Yep.

SELMA: And I am still here.

ELKA: Yep.

SELMA: I thought I heard Mark.

ELKA: Yes, you heard right, but he went to get a coffee.

SELMA: I want to see him.

ELKA: Chatting with a pretty nurse is more fun than dealing with a hysterical wife. I don't blame him, to be honest.

SELMA: You can't make me jealous.

ELKA: It's the truth.

SELMA: And I am not hysterical.

ELKA: Whatever.

SELMA: You are like a cat that kills its prey slowly.

ELKA: What happened to my little mouse? Weren't we getting along just fine?

SELMA: I want this to stop.

ELKA: Then stop keeping me here.

SELMA: I did everything you wanted and I still can't see my baby.

ELKA: Oh, the baby boy.

SELMA: My son.

ELKA: You are so sure it's a son.

SELMA: You said it was.

ELKA: You believe everything I say.

SELMA: Please go away. Let me be!

ELKA: My dear, I have better places to go than Homerton Hospital, but I am as trapped as you are right now.

SELMA: I've never felt this helpless.

Pause.

SELMA: I had this dream once. I'm in my primary school, but the school is invaded by soldiers. I find a fire escape to run away. I grab my mum's hand, but my mum doesn't want to go with me. She wants to stay with my little brother; apparently I have a little brother in my dream. Somehow I understand her position and allow her to make her choice. While we discuss this, the soldiers are coming closer and closer. I run up the stairs to get out, leaving my mum there. Then Hitler himself is chasing me. He grabs at my feet as I climb. At some point I kick him on the head and watch him tumble down right to the bottom. I think, that's it, I'm definitely dead now, if they catch me. I've just kicked Hitler on the head. Then I manage to open the door and there's a hill. I start climbing, but the hill is a sand dune and my feet can't get a grip. Next, I'm in the camp. It's a big warehouse. I see a group of people who have covered themselves with burkas from top to bottom, huddling together, trying to hide. They look like black bin bags, really. I am watching them from somewhere above, like from a balcony, not knowing where to go. I find them ridiculous, because there's no place to hide in the camp. Cameras are everywhere. Then I notice a little shop on the corner. I suddenly want a Mars bar, which I wouldn't eat in normal life. A black soldier starts shooting as I get closer to the shop. I tell him: 'But, you can't be a Nazi. You're black!' He tells me that he is just doing his job. I wake up, crying hysterically.

ELKA: Dreams are powerful things.

SELMA: We always say 'I have my dreams'. 'My future is built on my dreams'. 'My dreams came true'. Somehow I don't want to dream anymore.

ELKA: Dreams are part of life.

SELMA: They always seem far away. Good dreams are so rare.

SCENE 6

MARK is back with two coffees.

MARK: I didn't put any sugar in.

CLAIRE: Ah, that's alright. I'm sweet enough.

It's lovely. How much do I owe you?

MARK: Nothing.

CLAIRE: Oh, thanks.

MARK: No problem. Did she wake up?

SELMA: Coffee. I smell coffee.

ELKA: Coffee was forbidden in my day.

CLAIRE: Still sleeping like a baby.

MARK: Selma loves coffee.

SELMA: Why?

ELKA: Humans always find something to forbid. Especially when it comes to women.

SELMA: Oh, it smells so good.

CLAIRE: I am trying to give up, but to do long shifts without coffee is unthinkable.

SELMA: If I just take one sip.

ELKA: They used to say, if you drink coffee the devil gets into you.

MARK: Selma gave up everything before she got pregnant, but she always had a weakness for coffee. The smell of it drives her crazy.

CLAIRE: It is evil I tell you.

SELMA: Mark!

MARK: I'm a tea person.

CLAIRE: We have tea here, if you prefer tea.

SELMA: Mark!

MARK: I thought I could share it with Selma, if she wakes up.

CLAIRE: Coffee would make her more agitated.

SELMA: Why is he ignoring me?

ELKA: I don't know, but don't expect me to call him for you.

SELMA: I wouldn't expect anything from you.

CLAIRE: It makes me hyper.

ELKA: Relax!

SELMA: Why don't you just shut up!

ELKA: A wife on the verge of insanity.

SELMA: You're the one driving me to it.

CLAIRE: The more I get hyper the more I want to drink.

MARK: It's insane.

ELKA: Wouldn't you prefer insanity sometimes?

SELMA: I just want a sip of coffee to get my energy back and go to the bloody toilet.

CLAIRE: What?

MARK: I thought I heard Selma.

SELMA: I need to piss so badly.

ELKA: Piss then.

SELMA: How would I face the nurse?

ELKA: Burst your bladder then, see if I care.

MARK: Selma drank so much coffee once she was twitching all evening. To clear it from her system, she drank tons of water and she wet the bed that night. Guilty, like a little cat, she said: 'Mark, I just pissed myself. Please, could you change the bedding?'

CLAIRE: Ooooh! Did you?

MARK: Of course I did.

SELMA: I don't believe he said that to a stranger. That's a very private thing.

MARK: I sometimes think that women test men to find out if they're right for certain tasks.

SELMA: I just need to piss.

CLAIRE: We women need to know everything about our men.

SELMA: Don't agree with him, you silly cow.

ELKA: See how easily women in your time give in to a little chat?

CLAIRE: How did you meet your wife?

SELMA: I don't believe this.

ELKA: Women would have been whipped in my time, if they talked to a man like that.

MARK: Oh, it's a long story.

SELMA: Thank God we're not in your time.

CLAIRE: I bet it was really romantic.

ELKA: She's just bored.

SELMA: Please, look at me!

CLAIRE: I love to hear other people's love stories.

SELMA: Mark, do me a favour. Please, change the subject.

MARK: How long have you been a nurse?

SELMA: He heard me. He heard me.

ELKA: *(Imitating SELMA.)* He heard me. He heard me.

SELMA: I'm starting to think that you're a bit jealous.

ELKA: Oh, please.

SELMA: You are, aren't you?

CLAIRE: Two weeks ago it was my fifth year. I celebrated with my mates from work. We got completely hammered.

ELKA: A bit perhaps.

SELMA: Why?

ELKA: Because, I wasn't allowed to do any of the things you do now. I always did things in secret. So many things were forbidden to us.

MARK: Where did you go?

CLAIRE: Oh, the pub on the corner. We always go there at the weekend just to get rid of the long hours and stress.

MARK: Do you like it?

ELKA: 'Don't eat lamb's heart, your hair won't grow'.

CLAIRE: Drinking with my mates?

ELKA: 'Don't eat brain or liver, you'll be dumb'.

MARK: No, your job.

SELMA: I understand forbidding coffee is unreasonable.

CLAIRE: Pays the bills.

ELKA: To forbid something to some and not to others, makes that thing like a forbidden lover that you must have.

MARK: So you don't enjoy it.

CLAIRE: I don't know.

SELMA: We intoxicate our system with so much junk. Sometimes I see people on the street with red faces, full of acne and blisters, and I just think they look like a barrel

of radioactive stuff ready to explode; and if they do, their
blood will be yellow or green.

MARK: Did you ever think of doing something else?

SELMA: What, he's trying to change her life now?

CLAIRE: Like what?

SELMA: He'll tell her to study law in a second.

MARK: I don't know; become a doctor perhaps?

ELKA: To you, changing jobs is like changing a pair of jeans.

CLAIRE: Oh, I wouldn't like to be a doctor.

MARK: Why not?

SELMA: He's not going to give up, is he?

ELKA: I couldn't even have dreamed of having a job.

CLAIRE: Too much responsibility.

MARK: Perhaps law then.

SELMA: I knew it.

ELKA: Too many women are still in my position.

CLAIRE: What's wrong with being a nurse?

MARK: Absolutely nothing.

SELMA: Why is it your concern then?

MARK: You're still young. You can try other things while there
are still possibilities.

ELKA: That's what went wrong with modern societies. Too
many choices.

SELMA: I know you've been around for thousands of years,
but don't think you're in a position to analyse our society.

CLAIRE: I want to do some travelling.

ELKA: See what I'm trying to say?

MARK: Something everyone must do. Selma always wanted to travel.

SELMA: I never had the chance.

CLAIRE: What's stopping her?

SELMA: Why don't they talk about something else?

ELKA: About what?

SELMA: I don't know, books perhaps?

MARK: So, how is it doing night shifts?

CLAIRE: Oh, it can be really manic, but sometimes I end up chatting with charming men like you.

ELKA: This is going somewhere.

SELMA: Shut up.

MARK: I thought you made an exception just for me.

CLAIRE: People always push the rules.

MARK: Selma hates rules. She doesn't let anything in her way when she wants something.

CLAIRE: I know. She nearly knocked me over.

ELKA: He thinks you're a dictator.

SELMA: When I want to do something useful and right.

CLAIRE: She has such a gentle face.

MARK: She can be really tough sometimes.

CLAIRE: Really?

ELKA: I'm really enjoying this!

SELMA: Mark, don't do this.

MARK: When she is upset, she is really upset.

CLAIRE: We all get upset from time to time.

MARK: Oh, with Selma it can go on for days.

ELKA: Ha! You are still that stubborn little girl.

SELMA: I am not.

MARK: She can be really annoying.

SELMA: He doesn't know how annoying he gets himself.

CLAIRE: Marriage.

MARK: Sometimes I wish I could dissect her brain and find out how she wraps her thoughts inside that skull.

ELKA: Well, well, well.

SELMA: There are ways to reach my thoughts.

ELKA: He is a rocket ready to take off.

SELMA: If you know how to listen sometimes.

CLAIRE: But you love your wife.

ELKA: Do you think he loves you?

SELMA: Mark, please hold me!

ELKA: He doesn't hear you.

SELMA: Mark!

ELKA: You better print this in that little skull of yours.

MARK: A few weeks ago she was in one of her funny moods again. It went on for days. I thought this time we're done. Fuck this. This is not the way I want to live my life.

ELKA: Did you know this?

SELMA: I don't know anything anymore.

CLAIRE: What did you do?

MARK: I was ready to walk out and forget everything. I mean everything.

ELKA: Forget you and your son.

SELMA: Why is he doing this to me? Mark, what are you saying?

MARK: I woke up with her drying her hair. She has to dry her hair every morning. It drives me crazy.

SELMA: I knew he hated that. I will shave it off. You'll see.

CLAIRE: Has she tried wearing her hair short?

ELKA: Why don't you shave it then?

SELMA: He likes it long.

MARK: I got up and took the hair dryer from her, ready to smash it on the mirror for everyone's peace and quiet; but I didn't. Instead, I held it for her and she dried her hair. Then, she gave me this hug full of emotion and I felt a glacier was melting in my chest. She was like a little sparrow looking for a warm place.

CLAIRE: I'm glad you didn't smash the hair dryer.

ELKA: Or your brain for that matter.

CLAIRE: You haven't told me how you two met yet.

ELKA: He should have brought the wedding photos with him.

SELMA: I wouldn't be surprised.

MARK: She was singing for a charity, raising money for one of those human rights groups and I was invited by one of my clients, whom I quite fancied at the time.

CLAIRE: What do you do?

ELKA: She's keen to hear all about him.

SELMA: I want to go home!

MARK: I'm a lawyer.

CLAIRE: And your wife is a singer. Completely opposite.

MARK: In her heart, yes, but that's not what she chose to do.

ELKA: Stupid girl.

MARK: She works for the NHS, believe it or not.

CLAIRE: Really?

MARK: In a clinic. She's the General Manager.

ELKA: Boring.

MARK: Of course, I didn't know she was working for the NHS then.

CLAIRE: You thought she was a singer.

MARK: I thought she was an angel dropped from heaven.

ELKA appears on SELMA's bed, she pulls a red drape from beneath the mattress. Light changes. SELMA cradles the red drape. At first SELMA cannot sing. She is almost wailing, but then she sings a lament. Music changes into something more lively. ELKA leads SELMA into a dance. ELKA wraps the drape around SELMA like an umbilical cord and twists her, they start spinning around, SELMA dances faster and faster. ELKA moves away, taking the red drape with her. SELMA returns to bed through her movement, lies down like a baby, exhausted.

Lights down.

SCENE 7

MARK is sleeping on the chair in the waiting room. CLAIRE watches him.

MARK: How long have I been sleeping?

CLAIRE: Shshsh… Two hours.

MARK: What?

CLAIRE: Kidding. Only a few minutes.

MARK: I thought I heard Selma.

CLAIRE: She woke up briefly. Still a bit restless, but she went back to sleep again.

MARK: I wish you'd woken me up.

CLAIRE: You were sleeping. I didn't want to disturb the peace. She knows you're here.

MARK: You think so? You're very nice.

CLAIRE: It's OK.

MARK: Thank you for listening to me. I'm sorry.

CLAIRE: It's OK.

MARK: It's not OK.

MARK bursts into tears and sobs.

It's bloody hell.

She helps him to sit.

CLAIRE: Would you like some water?

MARK: Yes, please.

CLAIRE brings him some water.

MARK: I'm sorry.

CLAIRE: You have nothing to be sorry about. Have you thought about taking him home?

MARK: Home?

CLAIRE: Giving him a proper burial.

MARK: No, I haven't.

CLAIRE: Some couples do the full ceremony. I can get the hospital to make the arrangements if you'd like.

MARK: I don't know. I'll ask Selma.

CLAIRE: Whatever you prefer.

MARK: Thank you.

SELMA: Where did you disappear to?

ELKA: I think she's falling for your husband.

SELMA: I thought you were gone.

ELKA: I don't believe this. Did you miss me?

SELMA: We danced.

ELKA: You liked that, didn't you? I knew a woman a long time ago who was stoned to death for wearing a red dress. On her deathbed, she said 'Take my dress, and give it to another woman who could wear it proudly'. I promised and said 'I will take it to every corner of the world'. She smiled and said 'Keep me alive.' And those were her very last words.

SELMA: Sometimes I think the human race is a bit lost.

ELKA: Like me, you mean.

SELMA: It's natural for other species to survive, but I don't understand how we humans do.

ELKA: Simple. We breathe, we eat, we drink.

SELMA: We have a conscience.

ELKA: What's your point?

SELMA: As long as we have a conscience, we recognise guilt. If we feel guilty, then perhaps we are put in this world to change it.

ELKA: Listen, any nest can be blown away by a strong wind. But that doesn't stop the bird re-building it next year.

SELMA: I'm tired.

ELKA: How do you think I feel?

SELMA: I want to stay with my boy. Please, take me with you.

ELKA: Run if you can, to survive. Never run from life.

ELKA puts a tiny flower in SELMA's hair. She leaves.

SELMA: I'm ready to go.

MARK hears SELMA and goes to her.

MARK: I'm glad you are.

SELMA: Where is she?

SELMA tries to get up. MARK helps her.

MARK: Easy.

SELMA: I think I wet the bed.

MARK: Do you want me to call for the nurse?

SELMA: No, please don't.

MARK: That's OK. I won't.

He helps her change her clothes. She now sits on the bed. They don't talk.

MARK: The nurse said that we can leave whenever you're ready. She can bring you something to eat if you'd like.

SELMA: I don't think I can eat anything right now.

MARK: We'll go home then.

SELMA: I'm sorry.

SELMA starts crying. MARK holds her.

MARK: You shouldn't be. We'll try again.

SELMA: Aren't you tired of trying?

MARK: Life is already tiring without a baby. I can't imagine how tiring it will be with one. I'm not in a hurry.

He strokes her hair. He finds the dry flower.

MARK: What's this?

SELMA: It's Elka.

SELMA takes the flower, smells it, and puts it in her hair, smiling. CLAIRE approaches.

CLAIRE: How're you feeling?

SELMA: Thank you for looking after me and Mark.

CLAIRE: Oh, you are welcome. Have you decided what you're going to do?

MARK: No, we haven't talked about it yet.

CLAIRE: Let me know if there's anything I can do for you.

MARK: Thank you.

Pause.

SELMA: Do we need to sign anything?

MARK: We can take the body home and give him a proper burial if you'd like.

SELMA: No.

MARK: I know it won't make you feel any better, but…

SELMA: We never did that before.

MARK: The nurse thinks it might be better if we…

SELMA: No. I don't want that.

MARK: OK. OK. If that's what you want.

SELMA: Thank you.

MARK: Are you ready?

SELMA: Yes.

They leave.

Lights down.

BY THE SAME AUTHOR

SILVER BIRCH HOUSE
9781840027877

In a remote mountain village in eastern Turkey, against a backdrop of mounting political turmoil, a father clings to the simple life he has created for himself and his family.

As violence creeps ever closer, Haydar refuses to flee from the family home, a home he built with his bare hands. What keeps him here? Why do his silver birch trees seem more precious to him than the lives of his own children?

WWW.OBERONBOOKS.COM

Follow us on www.twitter.com/@oberonbooks
& www.facebook.com/oberonbook